THE NCAA JOKE BOOK

by Stevie Jay

for additional copies call
1-800-424-JOKE
THEODORE BOOKS 1990

*"BETTER TO BE A MAN IN THE
MOUTH OF A LION, THAN A
UNIVERSITY IN THE HANDS
OF THE NCAA"*

THE NCAA JOKE BOOK
A THEODORE BOOK/DECEMBER 1990
ALL RIGHTS RESERVED

THEODORE PUBLISHING
CALL 1-800-424-JOKE TO ORDER

PRINTED IN THE UNITED STATES OF AMERICA

INTRODUCTION

I suppose frustration can be credited with the writing of this book. For 17 months, the NCAA investigated the University of Illinois. After withstanding the entire ordeal, there was no feeling of justice, no feeling of fair treatment. Even as they read the sanctions, the NCAA seemed to make it a point to say that, regardless of the "no finding" ruling on the major allegations, they believed them to be true. After observing all of this as a fan, it's shockingly evident that the NCAA process has nothing to do with justice. It has nothing to do with the way we in America have come to expect to be treated. At this writing, I believe the NCAA investigative process is absolutely unfair and only those who have experienced it can truly understand. No matter what a university is accused of, truth and justice should be the prevailing goal, not vindictive rhetoric. Fortunately, we live in a country where we can still laugh and poke fun at authority. I'm thankful for that. My hope is that sooner rather than later, the process will be changed. It's long overdue. I hope you enjoy this book and maybe it can relieve some tension through laughter, truly the best medicine.

Steven Jay Khachaturian
Champaign, Illinois 1990

ACKNOWLEDGMENTS

To Doug Abbott and Brandon Griffing, I appreciate your help. And to Bill Mellberg, truly the best presidential impressionist in America, thanks for your creative input. Thanks to my brother Jon whose wisdom and guidance I depend on, and to my wife Janet, whose love, support and enthusiasm makes life fun every single day.

DEDICATION

This is for everyone who has experienced the NCAA Enforcement Process ... for now you understand.

HOW MANY NCAA ENFORCEMENT
OFFICIALS DOES IT TAKE TO QUESTION
A WITNESS?
seven — 2 to ask questions ... 3 to
hold them down ... and 2 to change
their answers

WHY DOES THE NCAA TAPE EVERY
PHONE CALL INTO THEIR OFFICE?
you just never know what you can
edit together

WHAT IS THE NCAA'S IDEA OF MERCY?
not laughing while they read your
sanctions

WHEN DO NCAA STAFFERS GO
BOWLING?
whenever they need new shoes

WHAT EVER HAPPENED TO THE
PERSON IN CHARGE OF THE
WATERGATE TAPES?
  they're in charge of audio at the ncaa

WHAT IS THE DIFFERENCE BETWEEN A
BEER AND THE NCAA?
  the beer has a head

WHAT DO YOU CALL 2 NCAA
ENFORCEMENT STAFF MEMBERS AT
THE BOTTOM OF THE OCEAN?
  a good beginning

WHY WON'T A HORNET STING AN
NCAA ENFORCEMENT STAFF MEMBER?
  professional courtesy

HOW DOES THE NCAA SPELL NOT
GUILTY?
n-e-v-e-r

HOW MANY NCAA ENFORCEMENT
OFFICIALS DOES IT TAKE TO SCREW IN
A LIGHT BULB?
they don't know how to screw in a
light bulb

WHAT DOES IT TAKE TO GET A JOB
WITH THE NCAA?
an internship with Saddam Hussein

HOW CAN YOU TELL THE NCAA IS
LYING?
whenever they open their mouth

WHY DO ENFORCEMENT OFFICIALS
RIDE BICYCLES BACKWARDS?
    don't they do everything that way?

WHAT IS THE OFFICIAL TOOL OF THE
NCAA ENFORCEMENT STAFF?
    white out

WHAT DID THE NCAA RULE AFTER
INVESTIGATING FLORIDA?
    guilty

DID YOU KNOW RICHARD NIXON WAS
OFFERED THE EXECUTIVE
DIRECTORSHIP AT THE NCAA?
    he turned it down because it was too
    crooked

NCAA OFFICIAL: people must think we're perfect idiots
UNIVERSITY OFFICIAL: you'll never be perfect

WHAT'S THE DIFFERENCE BETWEEN THE AVERAGE AGE OF AN NCAA ENFORCEMENT STAFFER AND THEIR AVERAGE IQ?
    the age is always higher

WHAT'S THE MOTTO OF THE NCAA?
    we get mad ... you get had

WHY CAN'T YOU TAR AND FEATHER AN NCAA ENFORCEMENT STAFF MEMBER?
    tar won't stick to something that slimy

HOW DOES THE NCAA SPELL JUSTICE?
  anyway they want

in a phone call to a University:
NCAA OFFICIAL: "this is the nc-double-a calling."
university official: "who?"
NCAA OFFICIAL: "that'll cost you."

WHY DON'T NCAA ENFORCEMENT STAFF MEMBERS EAT AT FAST FOOD RESTAURANTS?
  because nothing the ncaa does is fast

HOW DOES THE NCAA SPELL LOYAL?
  f-i-n-k

WHAT DOES THE NCAA AND PERRY MASON HAVE IN COMMON?
  they've never lost a case

WHAT DOES THE NCAA PROCESS HAVE
TO DO WITH A COURT OF LAW?
 nothing

DID YOU HEAR THE NCAA HAS A NEW
900 NUMBER SO YOU CAN CALL TO
GET INFORMATION ON WHO'S NEXT
TO BE INVESTIGATED?
 it's 1-900-NO-MERCY

WHAT IS THE NCAA'S FAVORITE
SONG?
 "my way"

WHAT IS THE NCAA'S FAVORITE
MOVIE?
 "the terminator"

HOW DOES THE NCAA SPELL
CONVICTION?
    h-a h-a

WHY IS SANTA CLAUS SO RUSHED
CHRISTMAS EVE?
    he has to check with the ncaa to
    make sure potential athletes don't get
    toys

WHAT'S THE DIFFERENCE BETWEEN
GEORGE BUSH AND THE NCAA?
    george bush has to answer to
    someone

WHAT DOES NAZI GERMANY AND THE
NCAA HAVE IN COMMON?
    everything

WHY DO NCAA STAFFERS ALWAYS
WEAR A COAT AND TIE?
    they can always LOOK intelligent

WHY WON'T A SKUNK SPRAY AN
NCAA STAFF MEMBER?
    professional courtesy

WHERE WOULD YOU MOST LIKELY SEE
A PICTURE OF AN NCAA
ENFORCEMENT STAFFER?
    in a post office

WHY DO MEMBERS OF THE NCAA
ENFORCEMENT STAFF ALWAYS RIDE
FIRST CLASS?
    royalty always rides first class

WHY DON'T NCAA STAFFERS VISIT
PRISONS?
   once you're paroled … who goes
   back to visit?

WHY ARE NCAA STAFFERS SUCH
GOOD FISHERMEN?
   they get lots of practice hooking,
   reeling, and clubbing

WHAT'S THE DIFFERENCE BETWEEN A
DEAD SNAKE IN THE ROAD AND A
DEAD NCAA ENFORCEMENT STAFFER
IN THE ROAD?
   there are skid marks in front of the
   dead snake

WHY DO NCAA STAFFERS MAKE BAD
REFEREES?
   because referees have to be fair

WHAT DID ONE WITNESS SAY TO THE
NCAA ENFORCEMENT STAFF?
   whatever they wanted him to say

WHY DO NCAA REPORTS TAKE SO
LONG?
   because it takes a long time to look
   up every single word in the
   dictionary

WHY DO NCAA STAFFERS SPIT IN A
FAN?
   they have to bathe somehow

WHAT DID THE NCAA RULE AFTER
INVESTIGATING MARYLAND?
   guilty

WHO'S HAPPIEST WHEN NCAA
ENFORCERS COME TO TOWN?
 sewer rats ... it's not every day they
 see relatives

WHAT DOES AN ELEVATOR AND THE
NCAA HAVE IN COMMON?
 they both love a good shaft

HOW IS THE NCAA LIKE A BAD MEAL?
 both can make you sick

WHAT ARE THE NCAA RULES?
 simple ... just do what they say

WHAT DO NCAA OFFICIALS AND
SHARKS HAVE IN COMMON?
 both love waiting for a good kill

WHAT DO THEY TEACH YOU ABOUT
THE NCAA IN LAW SCHOOL?
   nothing

WHY IS THE NCAA LIKE A MULE?
   most people refer to them as asses

WHY DOES IT TAKE 3 NCAA STAFFERS
TO EAT OPOSSUM?
   2 do the eating while the other
   watches for headlights

HOW DOES THE NCAA LOOK AT THE
UNIVERSITY'S SIDE OF THE STORY?
   with a blindfold

HOW DOES THE NCAA LISTEN TO THE
UNIVERSITY'S SIDE OF THE STORY?
   with earplugs

IF A UNIVERSITY IS A CANDLE, WHAT
IS THE NCAA?
   the wind

HOW ARE NCAA STAFFERS LIKE DOGS?
   they both salivate

WHAT DOES THE NCAA SHARE WITH
A SHORT SIGHTED HORSE WITH
BLINDERS?
   tunnel vision

HOW IS THE NCAA LIKE A GAME OF
TENNIS?
   both couldn't survive without a racket

WHAT DID THE NCAA RULE AFTER
INVESTIGATING UNLV?
   guilty

WHAT IS THE DIFFERENCE BETWEEN
THE NCAA AND THE MAFIA?
    the mafia has a heart

WHAT DID THE MAFIA GODFATHER
SAY TO THE NCAA ENFORCEMENT
STAFFER?
    I wish I could be like you

HOW IS A FRAYED PLUG LIKE THE
NCAA ENFORCEMENT PROCESS?
    it's a matter of time before they short
    circuit

WHY WILL NCAA ENFORCEMENT
STAFFERS ONLY WATCH SESAME
STREET?
    it's the only show they can
    understand

WHO TRAINS THE NCAA
ENFORCEMENT STAFF?
   no one

WHO DOES THE NCAA CALL ON WHEN
THEY NEED A TACTFUL, NON
OFFENSIVE WAY TO WORD PRESS
RELEASES?
   Salmon Rushdie

HOW IS A WATCHMAKER LIKE THE
NCAA?
   both want to clean your clock

WHY DOES IT SEEM LIKE THE NCAA
ONLY INVESTIGATES CERTAIN
PROGRAMS?
   because it's true

WHY DOES THE NCAA PENALIZE EVERY
SCHOOL THEY INVESTIGATE?
    why not?

HOW DOES THE NCAA SPELL
TORTURE?
    f-u-n

WHY WAS IT SUCH A SHAME WHEN A
BUS LOAD OF NCAA STAFFERS WENT
OVER A CLIFF?
    there were 3 empty seats

WHAT ARE THE RUSSIAN LETTERS FOR
NCAA?
    k-g-b

WHY DON'T NCAA ENFORCEMENT
STAFF MEMBERS WEAR HATS?
    they don't make them that big

WHICH ONE DOESN'T BELONG?
    SADDAM HUSSEIN
    MU'AMMAR EL QADDAFI
    NCAA ENFORCEMENT STAFF
    JOSEF STALIN
    ADOLPH HITLER
    trick question ... they all belong
    together

THE NCAA PENALTY FOR LAUGHING AT
A HEARING IS AN AUTOMATIC 5 YEAR
PROBATION ... IF IT WEREN'T FOR
THAT PENALTY ... THOSE INVOLVED
WOULD NEVER HEAR THE EVIDENCE.

AN NCAA ENFORCEMENT OFFICIAL WAS SEEN AT A FUNERAL IN A TOWN HE'D NEVER BEEN IN BEFORE ... ATTENDING THE FUNERAL OF SOMEONE HE DIDN'T KNOW ... WHEN ASKED WHY HE WAS THERE HE RESPONDED ... "I was just enjoying my day off."

WHY DON'T NCAA OFFICIALS GO WALKING IN THE WOODS?
    for anyone with a gun, they're fair game

WHAT DO MOST NETWORK TV SHOWS AND THE NCAA ENFORCEMENT STAFF HAVE IN COMMON?
    equal intelligence

UNIVERSITY OFFICIAL: did you hear about the jet plane that had to make a crash landing because birds got clogged in the engines?
UNIVERSITY COACH: really? who was on board?
UNIVERSITY OFFICIAL: ncaa enforcement staffers
UNIVERSITY COACH: oh ... those poor birds

WHAT DO BAD DENTISTS AND THE NCAA HAVE IN COMMON?
   they both love drilling for no reason

WHAT DO GEISHA GIRLS AND THE NCAA HAVE IN COMMON?
   both love walking all over you

WHAT DID THE NCAA RULE AFTER INVESTIGATING KANSAS?
   guilty

IN A SMALL WAY...WHAT DOES THE
NCAA HAVE TO DO WITH CHRISTMAS?
  ever hear of the grinch

WHAT'S THE DIFFERENCE BETWEEN
THE NCAA AND SCROOGE?
  scrooge had the ability to change

HOW MANY NCAA ENFORCEMENT
STAFF BRAINS WOULD IT TAKE TO
MAKE ONE POUND?
  all of them

WHY WON'T NCAA ENFORCEMENT
STAFFERS EVER STEP ON A
COCKROACH?
  professional courtesy

WHY DO PIT BULLS ALWAYS GROWL WHEN THEY SEE NCAA ENFORCEMENT STAFFERS?
    for them...it's like looking in a mirror

WHAT WAS THE NCAA RULING AFTER INVESTIGATING NORTH CAROLINA STATE UNIVERSITY?
    guilty

WHEN DO NCAA ENFORCEMENT STAFFERS CLENCH THEIR TEETH?
    only when they're awake

WHAT DAY OF THE YEAR DOES THE NCAA REALLY WORK ON PUBLIC RELATIONS?
    halloween, with their faces carved on pumpkins all over America ... they regard this as a high-visibility day

WHY IS A CROCK POT SIMILAR TO THE NCAA?
> one is a pot...the other, just a crock

WHAT'S BROWN AND BLACK AND LOOKS GOOD ON AN NCAA ENFORCEMENT STAFFER?
> a doberman

HOW CAN YOU TELL A ONE-EYED NCAA ENFORCEMENT STAFFER?
> the glass eye shows their warmth

WHY DON'T NCAA ENFORCEMENT STAFFERS EVER TAPE THEIR CONVERSATIONS WITH WITNESSES?
> because they might come too close to the truth

WHY ISN'T THE NCAA INTERESTED IN
GETTING AN ACCURATE ACCOUNT OF
WHAT THE WITNESS SAYS?
   accuracy has nothing to do with it

In school one day, little Tommy hit
another boy in the stomach.
TEACHER: tommy, why did you do that?
TOMMY: I heard he was going to steal
my milk money.
TEACHER: well, who told you that?
TOMMY: I don't know but I bet it's true!
TEACHER: someday you'll make a great
ncaa enforcement staffer.

WHAT KIND OF BOOK DOES THE NCAA
ENJOY THE MOST?
   non-fiction ... they produce enough
   fiction every day

WHAT CONSTITUTES A CREDIBLE
WITNESS?
> the ability to say what the ncaa wants
> to hear

WHAT DO PARATROOPERS AND THE
NCAA HAVE IN COMMON?
> people tell them to take a flying leap

WHAT DID THE NCAA RULE AFTER
INVESTIGATING CINCINNATI?
> guilty

WHEN'S THE BEST TIME TO HAVE AN
INTELLIGENT, FAIR CONVERSATION
WITH AN NCAA ENFORCEMENT
STAFFER?
> when they're asleep

WHY CAN'T NCAA ENFORCEMENT
STAFFERS TELL TIME?
> with the attention they pay to detail
> ... they can't tell which is the big
> hand and which is the little hand

WHY DOES THE NCAA FLY AROUND IN
THEIR OWN PRIVATE JET PLANE?
> because when you run the country,
> you get to have things like that

HOW DOES THE NCAA SPELL DEFEAT?
> i-m-p-o-s-s-i-b-l-e

WHAT DID THE NCAA STAFFER SAY
WHEN HE SAW THE COACH BANGING
HIS HEAD AGAINST THE BRICK WALL?
> success!!

HOW DOES THE NCAA LOOK AT CARS
AND THE NATIONAL MEDIA?
 as vehicles

WHAT IS REQUIRED READING FOR ALL
NCAA STAFFERS?
 "Mein Kampf" and "The Rise and Fall
 of The Third Reich"

HOW DOES THE NCAA VIEW THE
TRUTH?
 as unnecessary

WHY ARE NCAA STAFFERS IN A HABIT
OF ALWAYS LOOKING AT THE FLOOR?
 because that's where they expect
 universities to be bowing

WHAT DOES THE NCAA HAVE TO DO
WITH A NIGHTMARE?
    they're recurring

WHAT WAS THE NCAA RULING AFTER
INVESTIGATING THE UNIVERSITY OF
KENTUCKY?
    guilty

HOW DO NCAA ENFORCERS FUEL
THEIR CARS?
    they take off the gas cap and blow

WHAT DO NCAA STAFFERS SPIT?
    don't all dragons spit fire?

WHAT HAPPENS TO UNIVERSITIES IF
THEY CHALLENGE THE NCAA?
   like leaves in the Fall, they get
   burned

WHAT IS THE NCAA'S GOLDEN RULE?
   do unto others, enjoy, and don't get
   caught

WHY DON'T NCAA STAFFERS
EXCHANGE GIFTS?
   since they can't tape, there's no way
   to make the packages pretty

WHAT WAS THE NCAA RULING AFTER
INVESTIGATING THE UNIVERSITY OF
MISSOURI?
   guilty

HOW IS A HAM RADIO OPERATOR AND AN NCAA ENFORCEMENT STAFFER THE SAME?
both have their very own frequency

WHY DON'T NCAA STAFFERS EMPHASIZE THE IMPORTANCE OF EDUCATION?
because none of them have one

WHAT DO THE NEIGHBORS OF NCAA STAFFERS APPRECIATE THE MOST?
moving day

WHY ARE NCAA STAFFERS ALWAYS OUT FLYING KITES?
they're just doing what people tell them to do

WHY DO NCAA ENFORCEMENT
STAFFERS LIKE UFO SIGHTINGS?
    there doesn't have to be proof ...
    they like that

WHAT WILL IT TAKE TO STOP THE
NCAA?
    armageddon

WHY WON'T NCAA STAFFERS CLIMB
TREES?
    because they lose too many scales
    on the branches

WHY DO SCORPIONS STAY AWAY
FROM NCAA STAFFERS?
    hey...they have a reputation to
    protect

WHILE ATTENDING A BASKETBALL
GAME AT A MAJOR UNIVERSITY:
1st NCAA STAFFER: boy, this team sure
is good
2nd NCAA STAFFER: after these crummy
comp seats, they won't be for long

WHAT'S THE NCAA ENFORCEMENT
STAFFER'S IDEA OF A GOOD DIET?
    about 2 universities a month

WHAT DOES A PICTURE HAVE IN
COMMON WITH THE NCAA?
    both love a good frame

WHAT GIFT DOES THE NCAA GIVE THE
UNIVERSITY TO REMEMBER THEM BY?
    a boomerang

WHY DO NCAA STAFFERS DESPISE
WEEKENDS?
> universities are closed

WHY DO NCAA STAFFERS BUY
PANTYHOSE?
> wearing them over their heads is
> often part of the uniform

WHY AREN'T NCAA STAFFERS EVER
INVITED TO EXPLAIN THEIR JOB AT A
SCHOOL'S CAREER DAY?
> they don't know what they do, how
> can they explain it to others?

WHAT IS ON A TYPICAL NCAA
BUSINESS CARD?
> information they need someone to
> say for that particular case

WHAT IS THE ONLY THING THAT AN
NCAA ENFORCEMENT STAFFER IS
AFRAID OF?
    a stenographer

WHY MUST ALL NCAA ENFORCEMENT
STAFFERS HAVE A WORLD GLOBE ON
THEIR DESK?
    because it's only a matter of time ...

WHAT WAS THE NCAA RULING AFTER
INVESTIGATING CLEMSON?
    guilty

HOW IS AN NCAA ENFORCEMENT
STAFFER EVALUATED?
    by how many notches they have on
    their boots

HOW DOES THE NCAA SPELL BLAME?
    y-o-u

WHAT IS THE NCAA'S FAVORITE
FLOWER?
    the black orchid

WHY DON'T NCAA STAFFERS EVER
WEAR BRACES TO CORRECT CROOKED
TEETH?
    who needs straight teeth if you never
    smile?

WHERE DO MOST OF THE WORLD'S
DICTATORS GO ON VACATION?
    Overland Park, Kansas

WHY DOES THE NCAA PRIVATE JET
COME EQUIPPED WITH BOMBS?
you just never know when a
university has talked back once too
often

WHO'S THE MOST IMPRESSED WITH
THE NCAA?
the ncaa

WHY DON'T THE NCAA STAFFER AND
HIS DOG GET ALONG?
they eat out of the same bowl

WHY WON'T A RAT BITE AN NCAA
ENFORCEMENT STAFFER?
professional courtesy

WHAT DID THE NCAA RULE AFTER
INVESTIGATING OKLAHOMA?
   guilty

WHY DO NCAA STAFFERS USE LAMP
SHADES AS HATS?
   it's the only thing big enough to fit
   on their head

TWO DOGS ARE STANDING ON A
STREET CORNER WHEN THEY SEE AN
NCAA-OWNED DOG COMING. FIRST
DOG SAYS TO SECOND DOG: "BETTER
SIT DOWN, HERE COMES OLD 'COLD
NOSE'."

WHY IS A FOOTBALL LIKE THE NCAA?
   their heads are shaped the same

WHAT DID THE NCAA STAFFER'S BABY
DO AS SOON AS IT WAS BORN?
  it slapped the doctor

WHY ARE NCAA STAFFERS SO
SUPPORTIVE OF WILDLIFE?
  you tend to be sympathetic when
  you've been raised by wolves

HOW ARE BASKETBALL RIMS LIKE THE
HEADS OF NCAA STAFFERS?
  both are made of iron

WHAT IS THE DIFFERENCE BETWEEN A
BASEBALL AND AN NCAA STAFFER'S
HEAD?
  one has seams, the other has rivets

HOW IS AN NCAA ENFORCEMENT
STAFFER AND RONALD REAGAN
ALIKE?
    when it comes to answers from
    witnesses...they can't recall

WHY WON'T AN NCAA STAFFER EVER
CRACK AN EGG?
    you never know when there might be
    family inside

DID YOU HEAR ABOUT THE MARTIAN
SPACESHIP THAT LANDED AND PICKED
UP A HUMAN TO STUDY? THEY
CAPTURED AN NCAA ENFORCEMENT
STAFFER. TWO HOURS LATER, ONE
MARTIAN SAID TO THE OTHER..."I
THOUGHT YOU SAID THEY HAVE
BRAINS."

WHAT DOES JOAN OF ARC AND THE
NCAA HAVE IN COMMON?
one was burned at the stake ... the
other should be

WHY ARE NCAA ENFORCEMENT
STAFFERS SUCH FANS OF MARIE
ANTOINETTE?
they love making heads roll

THE NCAA WILL TELL YOU
EVERYTHING IT KNOWS, AND THEN
KEEP ON TALKING.

WHAT IS THE MOST COMMON WAY
NCAA STAFFERS LEAVE
RESTAURANTS?
one stays at the table while the other
two bring the car around

HOW IS A SHARP PENCIL DIFFERENT
FROM AN NCAA STAFFER'S
ARGUMENT?
> one has a point ... the other never
> does

HOW IS A GARAGE-DOOR OPENER AND
THE OUTCOME OF AN NCAA
INVESTIGATION THE SAME?
> they're both automatic

WHY DON'T NCAA ENFORCEMENT
STAFF MEMBERS LIKE TO FLY ON
COMMERCIAL AIRLINES?
> because whenever they're
> recognized, they're forced to jump

WHAT IS THE NCAA'S FAVORITE BIRD?
> the vulture

WHY DOES THE NCAA ALWAYS MAKE
IT A POINT TO SHAKE HANDS BEFORE
THEY LEAVE A UNIVERSITY?
    they're wearing a joy buzzer

HOW IS TISSUE PAPER AND AN NCAA
LETTER OF INQUIRY SIMILAR?
    both are useful when blowing your
    nose

WHY DO NCAA ENFORCEMENT STAFF
MEMBERS PREFER BLACK-AND-WHITE
TELEVISIONS?
    that's the way they see everything

WHEN AN NCAA ENFORCEMENT
STAFFER GOES TO THE PARK TO EAT,
WHY DOESN'T HE TAKE FOOD?
    he gets plenty thrown at him

HOW DO BIRDS SEE MEMBERS OF THE NCAA ENFORCEMENT STAFF?
    as target practice

HOW IS A PIECE OF BAD WOOD AND THE NCAA ALIKE?
    both are warped

WHAT DID THE NCAA RULE AFTER INVESTIGATING OKLAHOMA STATE?
    guilty

WHAT DO THEY DO AT NCAA STAFF PARTIES?
    instead of talking about the content of their official report, they talk about what really happened

WHAT IS AN NCAA ENFORCEMENT
STAFFER'S IDEA OF A GOOD TIME?
　　watching a good cock fight

WHY ARE NCAA COMPANY CARS
ALWAYS BLACK?
　　that's the only color hearses come in

HOW CAN YOU TELL WHO THE NCAA
ENFORCEMENT STAFFER IS WHEN
THEY COME TO YOUR CAMPUS?
　　they are the only ones wearing the
　　self-inscribed "S" on their chest

WHY DOES THE NCAA WANT MONEY
FROM ALL THE TIREMAKERS IN
AMERICA?
　　because they've left tread marks on
　　so many people

WHY DO MEMBERS OF THE NCAA
ENFORCEMENT STAFF WEAR
BULLETPROOF VESTS?
    wouldn't you?

WHY DOES THE NCAA ENJOY
WATCHING A FOOTBALL TEAM HIT
DIRTY?
    they understand it

IN A COURT OF LAW, WITNESSES ARE
REQUIRED TO TELL THE WHOLE TRUTH
AND NOTHING BUT THE TRUTH. HOW
DOES THE NCAA TELL ITS TRUTH?
    infractions

WHAT'S THE DIFFERENCE BETWEEN
THE NCAA AND A LOST TOURIST?
    you can tell a lost tourist where to go

WHAT DOES NCAA STAND FOR?
  no class at all

ON THEIR WAY TO UNIVERSITY TOWNS
FOR AN INVESTIGATION, WHAT DO
MEMBERS OF THE NCAA
ENFORCEMENT STAFFERS WATCH ON
THEIR PRIVATE JET?
  any blood sucking vampire movie ...
  it really gets them in the mood

NCAA STAFFER TO DOCTOR: doc,
what's wrong with me?
DOCTOR: physically, mentally or both?
NCAA STAFFER: both.
DOCTOR: how much time do you have?

WHY DID THE NCAA ADMINISTRATOR
TELL HIS STAFF THEY COULDN'T
UPDATE THEIR OFFICE EQUIPMENT?
  because then they would have to
  deal with the "fax"

WHAT IS THE DIFFERENCE BETWEEN
THE NCAA AND THE P.L.O.?
   you can usually negotiate with the
   P.L.O.

WHAT IS THE DIFFERENCE BETWEEN
THE NCAA ENFORCEMENT STAFF AND
THE BOY SCOUTS?
   boy scouts have adult leadership

THE NCAA ENFORCEMENT STAFF
NEVER HAS TO WORRY ABOUT BRAINS
BEING CONTAGIOUS. THEY ALL HAVE
IMMUNITY.

DID YOU HEAR ABOUT THE COACH
WHO DIED AND WENT TO HEAVEN? HE
WAS MET AT THE PEARLY GATES AND
SHOWN THE BEAUTIFUL PRACTICE
AND GAME FIELDS, TRAINERS WHO
COULD WORK TRUE MIRACLES,
REFEREES WHO NEVER MAKE A
MISTAKE, AND IDEAL WEATHER
CONDITIONS. THEN THE ANGEL TOOK
THE COACH AND, AS THEY WERE
APPROACHING A SET OF DOORS, SAID,
"WE HAVE TO BE QUIET AS WE PASS
BY." "WHY?" ASKED THE COACH.
"BECAUSE THE NCAA ENFORCEMENT
STAFFERS ARE IN THAT ROOM AND
THEY THINK THEY'RE THE ONLY ONES
HERE"

WHY WON'T NCAA ENFORCEMENT
STAFF MEMBERS CARRY BRIEFCASES?
nothing the ncaa does is brief

WHY ARE NCAA STAFF MEMBERS
CAREFUL NOT TO MAKE A MISTAKE AT
WORK?
> because they don't like getting hit on
> the nose with a rolled up newspaper

WHAT MOVIE'S MUSIC REALLY HITS
HOME FOR THE NCAA ENFORCEMENT
STAFF?
> the theme from "Jaws"

WHAT DID THE NCAA RULE AFTER
INVESTIGATING THE UNIVERSITY OF
ILLINOIS?
> guilty

WRITE YOUR OWN NCAA JOKES HERE: